CROCK-TOBER

VOLUMES 1 & 2

by

Laurie Hise

CONTENTS

FORWARD

Do you dream of getting dinner done and on the table, but find yourself overwhelmed while driving carpool, tackling laundry, helping out with homework and racing to the next event without a plan for dinner each night?

Then Crock-tober is just for you.

As a work-from-home wife and mom to three busy kids, I've made countless slow cooker meals to get dinner done in our home each and every week. In 2016 I turned our ordinary "October" into "Crock-tober", and the idea for this book was born.

To make your life easier, I've included grocery lists and menu plans each week. And since our first Crock-tober was a huge success, two volumes are included so you can mix and match the perfect menu plan for your family.

My hope is that this makes getting dinner done in your home more manageable each day, so that you feel empowered to take control of the dinner hour, spending more of your hard-earned dollars on whole foods instead of at the drive-thru.

A few helpful hints:

- A slow cooker and Crock-Pot® are the same thing. (Crock-Pot® is just a specific brand of slow cooker).

- Find the right size slow cooker - a slow cooker that's too large for your meal won't cook evenly so try to make sure to have the right size to ensure success. I typically use either a 4½ or 6 quart slow cooker for most recipes, and the recipes included in this book should all fit inside a 6 quart slow cooker easily.

- Fill your slow cooker no more than ¾ full.

- Choose the right cut of meat - I like shoulder roasts for beef, boneless skinless chicken breast, short ribs, pork shoulder and pork tenderloin best for slow cooker recipes.

- Plan ahead if you're able before heading out in the morning - chop your veggies the night before, set out your ingredients, and have your meat ready to go.

- The heat in your slow cooker comes from underneath the slow cooker, so you want to place items that take longest to cook (typically veggies like potatoes and carrots) on the bottom of your slow cooker.

- Layer your ingredients by adding root veggies first (carrots, potatoes, etc ~ making sure these are cubed prior to adding to the slow cooker), then other vegetables, then meat or poultry and lastly add in seasonings or sauce.

- Keep the lid on your slow cooker throughout the day.

- Most slow cooker recipes other than soups don't require very much liquid. Add the recommended liquids in the recipe but don't overdo it.

- To prevent food from sticking to your slow cooker, spray with cooking spray prior to cooking.

- Read ahead before grocery shopping to choose your side dishes for the week ~ while the main grocery list is prepared for you each week, you'll want to also pick up ingredients for salads, vegetables, and anything else you'd like as side dishes for each meal.

- The recipes make enough to serve 5 - 8 (depending on the ages of your children), and are all family approved.

- If you'd like, join our private Dinner's Done Facebook Group for extra dinner motivation and encouragement each day ~ http://bit.ly/2wUdVw9

Are you ready to get started and transform the dinner hour in your home? Let's dive in!

A very heartfelt thank you to so many readers of my blog, Passionate Penny Pincher, for joining me for our first Crocktober in 2016 and encouraging me to tackle a second round. I'm so incredibly thankful for each of you ~ you make my day, every day! Thanks also to the incredible PPP team who has done so much work to help me pull this together, there's no way this would ever have gotten done without you.

And, most importantly a big thanks to my sweet family for surviving exactly 5,739 slow cooker meals over the last 21 years (without too many complaints). :) You're what makes getting dinner done worth it each and every night ~ I'm so very thankful for you!

CROCK-TOBER

VOLUME 1

CROCK-TOBER

VOLUME 1 • WEEK ONE

WEEK ONE GROCERY LIST

PRODUCE
- ☐ 2 heads garlic
- ☐ 2 large onions
- ☐ 4 lbs potatoes

DAIRY
- ☐ 8 oz shredded Mexican four cheese, divided
- ☐ 3 cups mozzarella
- ☐ 1 stick butter or margarine
- ☐ 1½ cups milk

BUTCHER/DELI CASE
- ☐ 2-3 lb shoulder roast
- ☐ 3 lbs boneless, skinless chicken breasts, divided
- ☐ 1½ lbs ground beef or ground sausage
- ☐ 6 pork chops, ½ inch thick

DRY/CANNED GOODS
- ☐ 1 jar pepperoncini peppers
- ☐ 2 cans Rotel
- ☐ 3 15 oz cans white beans
- ☐ 2 4 oz cans chopped green chili peppers
- ☐ 2 10.75 oz cans cream of chicken soup (or homemade cream of chicken soup)
- ☐ 24 oz chicken broth
- ☐ 28 oz spaghetti sauce
- ☐ 1 packet Au Jus gravy mix
- ☐ 1 packet ranch salad dressing & seasoning mix (or homemade dry ranch dressing mix)
- ☐ 12 oz rigatoni pasta
- ☐ 1 package pepperoni

- ☐ 1 package hoagie rolls
- ☐ tortilla chips

PANTRY STAPLES
- ☐ salt
- ☐ pepper
- ☐ onion powder
- ☐ brown sugar
- ☐ cumin
- ☐ oregano
- ☐ cayenne pepper

OPTIONAL
- ☐ nacho fixin's (sour cream, green onions, black olives, lettuce and tomato)
- ☐ sliced mushrooms, black olives or onions (optional for Slow Cooker Rigatoni)
- ☐ salad blend for salads each night
- ☐ loaf Italian bread
- ☐ fresh, frozen, or canned veggies for side dishes

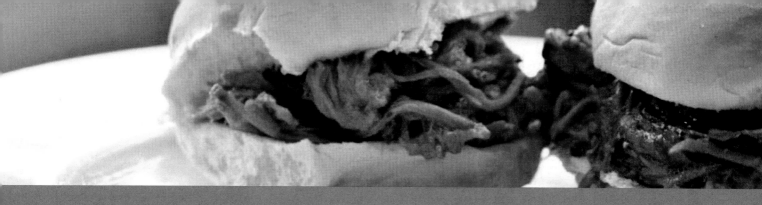

SLOW COOKER ITALIAN BEEF SLIDERS

2-3 lb	beef shoulder roast
1 jar	pepperoncini peppers, undrained
1 packet	Au Jus gravy mix
	hoagie rolls

1. Trim fat from roast. Place roast in slow cooker, cover with undrained pepperoncini peppers.
2. Cook 7-8 hours on low. Remove peppers (I usually save the jar in the morning and put the peppers back in it to throw them away).
3. Shred beef and mix in Au Jus gravy mix. If you want it to make it a little less spicy, drain about half the liquid using a turkey baster.
4. Cook another 30 minutes on low in slow cooker.
5. Serve on hoagie rolls.

daily grace

Lord Jesus, be our Guest –

our morning joy our evening rest.

And with our daily bread impart –

your love and peace to every heart.

SLOW COOKER CHICKEN NACHOS

3-4	boneless, skinless chicken breast
2 cans	Rotel, undrained
1 tsp	minced garlic
½ tsp	onion powder
½ tsp	salt
½ tsp	pepper
1½ Tbsps	brown sugar
	tortilla chips
¾ cup	shredded Mexican four cheese
	toppings: sour cream, green onions, black olives, lettuce and tomatoes (optional)

1. Mix together Rotel, garlic, onion powder, salt, pepper and brown sugar in a small bowl.

2. Place chicken in slow cooker and add Rotel mixture on top.

3. Cook 6-7 hours on low or 3-4 hours on high.

4. Shred chicken well.

5. Preheat oven to 350 degrees.

6. Arrange chips on the bottom of a large baking sheet.

7. Spoon chicken mixture over tortilla chips.

8. Top with cheese and tomato.

9. Bake for 10 minutes or until cheese has melted.

10. Top with extra toppings and serve.

SLOW COOKER RIGATONI

28 oz	spaghetti sauce
12 oz	rigatoni pasta, cooked al dente
1½ lbs	ground beef or ground sausage, cooked and drained
3 cups	shredded mozzarella
	pepperoni (optional)
	sliced mushrooms, black olives, or onion (optional)

1. Layer half of the spaghetti sauce in the bottom of the slow cooker.
2. Then add half the pasta, half the ground beef and half of the mozzarella cheese.
3. Layer pepperoni, mushrooms and/or black olives (optional).
4. Add another layer of all the ingredients.
5. Cook 3-4 hours on low and serve.

daily grace

Bless us with good food and laughter
may our love and joy be with us ever after.

SLOW COOKER RANCH PORK CHOPS

6	pork chops, ½ inch thick
1 packet	ranch salad dressing & seasoning mix (or homemade dry ranch dressing mix)
2 10.75 oz cans	cream of chicken soup (or homemade cream of chicken soup)
4 lbs	potatoes, peeled
5 Tbsps	butter or margarine
6	cloves roasted garlic
1½ cups	warm skim milk
1 Tbsp	salt to taste (optional)
1 tsp	fresh cracked pepper (optional)

PORK CHOPS

1. Place pork chops, ranch salad dressing & seasoning mix and soup in slow cooker. Cook 4 hours on high or 6 hours on low.

POTATOES

1. One hour before pork is finished, roast garlic. To roast the garlic, cover the entire garlic bulb including skin in aluminum foil and bake at 350 degrees for 1 hour. Let cool. Remove garlic from skins and mix into a paste to add to your potatoes.

2. While garlic is cooling, cook peeled potatoes in large pot of water for about 15-18 minutes, until ready to mash. Mash potatoes, then add butter or margarine, garlic, salt and pepper. Slowly add in milk until the potatoes are the consistency that you like them (about one cup of milk).

3. Add potatoes to plate, cover with pork chops from slow cooker and use sauce for gravy.

SLOW COOKER WHITE CHICKEN CHILI

1-1½ lbs	boneless, skinless chicken breast
3 15 oz cans	white beans, rinsed and drained
1	onion, chopped
3 cloves	garlic, crushed
2 4 oz cans	chopped green chile peppers
3 cups	chicken broth
1 tsp	cumin
1 tsp	oregano
1 tsp	cayenne pepper
1 cup	shredded Mexican four cheese

1. Place chicken, beans, onion, garlic, chiles and chicken broth in slow cooker.

2. Cook 6-8 hours on low or 3-4 hours on high.

3. After cooking, remove chicken breasts from slow cooker and shred meat.

4. Return meat to slow cooker and add in cumin, oregano and cayenne pepper. Let cook an additional 15-20 minutes.

5. Stir in Mexican four cheese until melted.

6. Serve with an extra sprinkle of cheese and sour cream if desired.

(If you feel like it needs a little more flavor, add in a seasoning packet of White Chicken Chili Seasoning Mix at the end of the day).

🌱 daily grace

Thank you for the world so sweet - thank you for the food we eat.

Thank you for the birds that sing - thank you Lord for everything.

CROCK-TOBER

VOLUME 1 • WEEK TWO

WEEK TWO GROCERY LIST

PRODUCE
☐ 2 large onions

DAIRY
☐ milk

BUTCHER/DELI CASE
☐ 3-4 lbs boneless skinless chicken breasts, divided
☐ 2 lbs ground beef
☐ 2-3½ lb shoulder roast
☐ 1 lb frozen meatballs

DRY/CANNED GOODS
☐ ½ cup beef broth
☐ 1 can beefy mushroom soup (NOT cream of mushroom)
☐ 1 can golden mushroom soup (NOT cream of mushroom)
☐ 10 oz hot sauce
☐ 28 oz jar spaghetti sauce
☐ 14½ oz can diced tomatoes
☐ 12 oz spaghetti noodles
☐ 1 jar salsa
☐ 1 packet taco seasoning mix (or homemade taco seasoning mix)
☐ 1 packet ranch salad dressing & seasoning mix (or homemade dry ranch dressing mix)
☐ prepared ranch dressing
☐ 1 package slider buns
☐ 1 package onion recipe soup & dip mix

☐ 1 package Au Jus gravy mix
☐ small package Italian seasoned bread crumbs

PANTRY STAPLES
☐ salt
☐ pepper
☐ flour
☐ kosher salt
☐ garlic powder
☐ minced garlic
☐ olive oil
☐ beef bouillon
☐ corn starch
☐ Italian seasoning
☐ Parmesan cheese

OPTIONAL
☐ taco fixin's (sour cream, green onions, black olives, lettuce and tomato)
☐ 5 lb bag of potatoes for mashed potatoes (optional with Slow Cooker Pot Roast and/or Slow Cooker Salisbury Steak)
☐ salad blend for salads each night
☐ fresh, frozen, or canned veggies for side dishes

11

SLOW COOKER POT ROAST

ROAST
2-3½ lb	shoulder roast
2 Tbsps	flour
1 tsp	kosher salt
½ tsp	black pepper
2 tsps	garlic powder
1 Tbsp	olive oil
1 medium	onion, sliced in rings
½ cup	beef broth
1 can	beefy mushroom soup (*NOT* cream of mushroom)

GRAVY
2 cups	broth from slow cooker
½ Tbsp	beef bouillon
¼ cup	water
2 Tbsps	corn starch

1. Trim all fat from roast.
2. Mix together flour, salt, pepper and garlic powder in large plastic bag.
3. Put roast in bag and shake it until completely coated in flour, then brown all sides in large skillet in olive oil.
4. While the meat is browning, add your onion slices to the bottom of the slow cooker.
5. Put roast on top of onions, then pour beef broth and soup over top. (If you want to add carrots or potatoes, you could also put those on top).
6. Cook 9 hours on low in slow cooker. Serve with mashed potatoes, veggies, and gravy.

GRAVY

1. Remove 2 cups of the broth and place in a saucepan over medium heat.
2. Add bouillon and stir until it's completely mixed into the broth.
3. Mix together 2 Tbsps corn starch and ¼ cup water.
4. Slowly add corn starch mixture to the broth, stirring constantly.
5. Simmer over medium heat for 1 minute. Season if needed.

🌱 daily grace
Bless the food before us -
the family beside us - and the love between us.

SLOW COOKER SPAGHETTI WITH MEATBALLS

1 lb	frozen meatballs
28 oz jar	spaghetti sauce
14½ oz can	diced tomatoes, undrained
1	large onion, diced
1 tsp	Italian seasoning
1 Tbsp	minced garlic
12 oz	spaghetti noodles
	Parmesan cheese

1. Put spaghetti sauce, undrained tomatoes, onion, garlic, and Italian seasoning in slow cooker.

2. Pour in frozen meatballs.

3. Cook 6-8 hours on low or 3-4 hours on high.

4. Before serving, cook spaghetti.

5. Serve sauce and meatballs over pasta ~ enjoy!

SKINNY SLOW COOKER CHICKEN TACOS

4-5	boneless, skinless chicken breasts
1½ cups	salsa
1 packet	taco seasoning mix (or homemade taco seasoning mix)
	toppings: lettuce, tomatoes, sour cream, shredded cheese (optional)

1. Place chicken in slow cooker and sprinkle taco seasoning over the top.

2. Pour salsa over chicken.

3. Cook 5-7 hours on low.

4. Shred meat and serve in taco shells, along with lettuce, tomatoes, sour cream and shredded cheese.

5. Enjoy!

daily grace
God our Father, Lord our Savior -
thank you for your love and favor.
Bless this food and drink we pray -
and all who shares with us today.

SLOW COOKER BUFFALO CHICKEN SLIDERS

1½ – 2 lbs	boneless, skinless chicken breast
10 oz	hot sauce
1 packet	ranch salad dressing & seasoning mix (or homemade dry ranch dressing mix)
1 package	dinner rolls
	ranch dressing for topping

1. Place chicken in slow cooker.

2. Mix together ranch salad dressing & seasoning mix and hot sauce, pour over the meat.

3. Cook 6-8 hours on low.

4. Shred chicken and slice buns in half.

5. Add chicken to buns and drizzle with ranch dressing to serve.

SLOW COOKER SALISBURY STEAK

2 lbs	ground beef
1 packet	onion recipe soup & dip mix
½ cup	Italian seasoned bread crumbs
¼ cup	milk
1 can	golden mushroom soup
1 packet	Au Jus gravy mix
1 ¼ cups	water

1. In medium bowl, mix together ground beef, onion recipe soup & dip mix, bread crumbs and milk.
2. Form into 8 patties.
3. In medium non-stick skillet, grill patties for just a minute to brown sides over medium high heat.
4. Place in slow cooker stacked in a pyramid shape.
5. Mix together golden mushroom soup, Au jus gravy mix and water.
6. Pour over meat in slow cooker.
7. Cook 3-4 hours on low, until meat is done.

daily grace
Oh Lord we thank thee for this food –
for every blessing – every good.
Be present at our table Lord – be here and everywhere adored.

CROCK-TOBER

VOLUME 1 • WEEK THREE

WEEK THREE GROCERY LIST

PRODUCE
- ☐ 3 large onions
- ☐ 2 green peppers
- ☐ 1 head garlic
- ☐ 2 stalks celery

DAIRY
- ☐ 2 10 oz cans inexpensive biscuits (store brand are fine)
- ☐ 8 oz cream cheese
- ☐ 8 oz lowfat cheddar or Colby cheese
- ☐ 6-8 slices provolone cheese

BUTCHER/DELI CASE
- ☐ 5-6 lbs boneless, skinless chicken breast, divided
- ☐ 3 lbs ground beef, divided

DRY/CANNED GOODS
- ☐ 3 10.75 oz cans cream of chicken soup (or homemade cream of chicken soup)
- ☐ 1 10 oz can chicken broth
- ☐ 1 packet taco seasoning mix (or homemade taco seasoning mix)
- ☐ 2 packets Italian salad dressing & recipe mix (or homemade Italian dressing mix)
- ☐ 12 oz dry pasta
- ☐ 24 oz beef broth
- ☐ 14 oz can chicken broth
- ☐ 1 can evaporated milk
- ☐ 6 hoagie buns

PANTRY STAPLES
- ☐ salt
- ☐ pepper
- ☐ garlic powder
- ☐ flour
- ☐ paprika

OPTIONAL
- ☐ salad blend for salads each night
- ☐ tortilla chips to add to cheeseburger soup
- ☐ fresh, frozen, or canned veggies for side dishes

SLOW COOKER CHICKEN & DUMPLINGS

1-2 lbs	boneless, skinless chicken breast
2 10.75 oz cans	cream of chicken soup (or homemade cream of chicken soup)
1 10 oz can	chicken broth
¼ cup	water
½ tsp	salt
½ tsp	garlic powder
¼ tsp	pepper
1	onion, chopped
2 10 oz cans	inexpensive biscuits cut in quarters

1. Place chicken breast, soup, broth, water, salt, garlic powder, pepper and onion in slow cooker.
2. Cook 6-7 hours on low.
3. 1 hour before dinner time, add quartered biscuits to slow cooker. (I use kitchen scissors to cut the biscuits).
4. Gently stir in biscuits so that they're covered.
5. Cook 1 more hour on low and serve.

daily grace

Thank you for the food we eat, and for every need You meet.
Keep our loved ones in your care, and all our blessings -
let us share.

TACO MEAT IN THE SLOW COOKER

2 lbs	ground beef
1 packet	taco seasoning mix (or homemade taco seasoning mix)
1 tsp	garlic powder
1 tsp	salt
¼ cup	onion, chopped
1½ cups	water

1. Place ground beef, water, onion, salt and garlic powder in slow cooker.
2. Cook about 2 hours on high, stirring occasionally (I stirred it twice throughout the day).
3. When meat is almost cooked through, stir again and turn your slow cooker down to low.
4. Cook an additional 1-2 hours.
5. Add in taco seasoning packet and give it a stir, then cook 20 more minutes.
6. Drain completely (will be a little liquidy from the water and some of the fat in the beef).
7. Serve over tacos and freeze any leftovers for up to 6 months.

SLOW COOKER CREAMY CHICKEN ALFREDO

1 lb	boneless, skinless chicken breast
1 can	cream of chicken soup (or homemade cream of chicken soup)
¼ cup	water
1 packet	Italian salad dressing & recipe mix (or homemade Italian dressing mix)
8 oz	cream cheese
12 oz	pasta (whatever type your family likes)

1. Place chicken, soup, water and Italian salad dressing & recipe mix in slow cooker.

2. Give it a quick stir, then cook 5-6 hours on low or 3-4 hours on high.

3. 30 minutes before serving, shred chicken and add in cream cheese. Give it another good stir to mix everything well.

4. Cook pasta according to package directions.

5. Once cream cheese is heated through and everything mixes together, give it one more stir.

6. Serve chicken and sauce over cooked pasta, top with Parmesan cheese.

daily grace

Come Lord Jesus, be our guest ~ may this food by You be blest.

May our souls by You be fed, ever on the Living Bread.

SKINNY SLOW COOKER CHEESEBURGER SOUP

	cooking spray
1 lb	ground beef
1 clove	garlic, minced
1 medium	onion, chopped finely
¼ cup	celery, chopped finely
2 Tbsps	all purpose flour
3 cups	beef broth
1 cup	evaporated milk
8 oz	low fat cheddar or Colby cheese
½ tsp	paprika
¼ tsp	table salt
1/8 tsp	black pepper
	baked low fat tortilla chips

1. Spray nonstick skillet with cooking spray and heat over medium high heat for 30 seconds.

2. Add onion, garlic and celery to skillet, cooking until vegetables are tender, about 5 minutes.

3. Spray slow cooker with cooking spray and pour in vegetables.

4. Add ground beef to the same skillet you used for the veggies and brown ground beef until cooked through.

5. Drain ground beef and add to slow cooker.

6. In small cup, mix together flour and ½ cup of the broth and stir until smooth.

7. Add flour and broth mixture to the skillet along with the remaining 2½ cups of broth.

8. Bring to a simmer, and stir well, including any of the browned bits in the slow cooker left from the beef ~ then transfer broth mixture to the slow cooker.

9. Add evaporated milk, cheese, paprika, salt and pepper to the slow cooker.

10. Cover and cook 2 hours on low.

11. Put a few chips in the bottom of your bowl then add soup and a few more crumbled chips and serve.

SLOW COOKER CHICKEN PHILLY CHEESESTEAK SANDWICHES

1½ lbs	boneless, skinless chicken breast
2	green peppers, sliced
1	onion, sliced
14 oz can	chicken broth
1 packet	Italian salad dressing & recipe mix (or homemade Italian dressing mix)
2 cloves	garlic
6	hoagie buns
6-8 slices	provolone

1. Place chicken in slow cooker.
2. Slice onions and peppers, pour on top of chicken.
3. Pour chicken broth over peppers, onions and chicken, then sprinkle Italian dressing packet over everything.
4. Cook 6 hours on low or 3-4 hours on high.
5. When ready to serve, open hoagie rolls, top with chicken and layer a slice of cheese on each side. Broil in oven for 1-2 minutes until lightly browned and cheese has melted.

daily grace
Thank You for the food we eat –
for bread and cheese, for milk and meat,
But, Lord we thank You most of all,
for warmth of friends who come to call.
To share our bread – our cup of cheer,
for friendship's always welcomed here.

CROCK-TOBER

VOLUME 1 • WEEK FOUR

PRODUCE
- ☐ 3 onions
- ☐ 3 cloves garlic
- ☐ 6 large peppers (preferably 4 green and 2 red)

DAIRY
- ☐ ½ stick margarine or butter

BUTCHER/DELI CASE
- ☐ 3-4 lbs boneless, skinless chicken breasts, divided
- ☐ 1-2 lbs chicken tenders
- ☐ 1 whole chicken
- ☐ 1½ lbs ground beef

DRY/CANNED GOODS
- ☐ 1 can cream of chicken soup (or homemade cream of chicken soup)
- ☐ 6 oz package stuffing mix
- ☐ 1 jar salsa
- ☐ 28 oz can crushed tomatoes
- ☐ 6 oz can tomato paste
- ☐ 2 packets fajita seasoning mix
- ☐ 16 10 inch flour tortillas
- ☐ 12 oz bottle chili sauce
- ☐ 12 oz package pasta
- ☐ 1 package hamburger buns

PANTRY STAPLES
- ☐ salt
- ☐ pepper
- ☐ cayenne pepper
- ☐ paprika
- ☐ onion powder
- ☐ garlic powder
- ☐ brown sugar
- ☐ Worcestershire
- ☐ Italian seasoning

OPTIONAL
- ☐ salad blend for salads each night
- ☐ fajita fixin's (sour cream, green onions, black olives, lettuce and tomato)
- ☐ fresh, frozen, or canned veggies for side dishes

SLOW COOKER CHICKEN & DRESSING

4 – 6	boneless, skinless chicken breasts
1 can	cream of chicken soup (or homemade cream of chicken soup)
1 ¼ cups	water
¼ cup	margarine, melted (can use less margarine to reduce fat content)
6 oz	package stuffing mix

1. Place chicken breast in slow cooker (frozen chicken breast is fine also, you may just want to add a little extra cooking time but I think it makes the meat more tender).

2. Pour soup on top of the chicken breast.

3. Mix together melted margarine and water. Stir in stuffing mix.

4. Pour stuffing mixture over the chicken and soup.

5. Cook 4 hours on low and serve.

daily grace

Thank you heavenly Father for all we eat and all we wear –
for daily bread and nightly care.

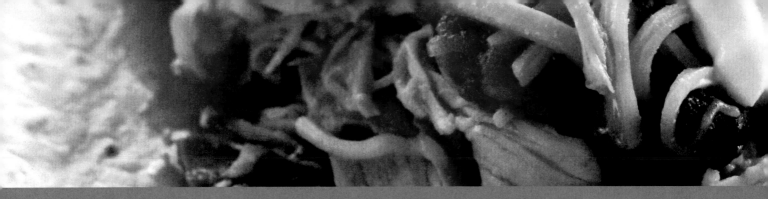

SLOW COOKER CHICKEN FAJITAS

2 lbs	boneless, skinless chicken breast
1	onion, sliced thinly
3 large	peppers (I used 2 green and one red), cut into strips
¾ cup	chunky salsa
2 packets	fajita seasoning mix
¼ tsp	cayenne pepper
16	10-inch flour tortillas
	toppings: shredded cheese, chopped tomatoes, sour cream, and guacamole (optional)

1. Put chicken in slow cooker.
2. Add onion and peppers.
3. In a bowl, mix salsa, fajita seasoning mix and cayenne pepper. Pour over chicken.
4. Cook 6-7 hours on low or 3-4 hours on high.
5. Shred chicken with a fork.
6. Serve over tortillas and add toppings. Save leftovers for chicken nachos or taco salad later in the week.

SLOW COOKER SLOPPY JOES

1½ lbs	ground beef
½ cup	chopped onion
½ cup	chopped red pepper
3 Tbsps	brown sugar
12 oz bottle	chili sauce
1 tsp	salt
1 Tbsp	Worcestershire sauce
	hamburger buns

1. Cook beef, onion and red pepper in skillet on medium heat until meat is cooked.
2. Add meat to slow cooker.
3. Add remaining ingredients (except hamburger buns) to slow cooker and cook 3-4 hours on low.
4. Serve over buns.

daily grace
Bless us oh Lord and these thy gifts
which we are about to receive from thy bounty –
through Christ our Lord, Amen.

SLOW COOKER CHICKEN CACCIATORE

1-2 lbs	frozen chicken tenders
1	onion, sliced
1	green pepper, sliced
1	red pepper, sliced
28 oz can	crushed tomatoes
6 oz can	tomato paste
3 cloves	garlic
1½ tsps	Italian seasoning
	salt and pepper to taste
1 lb	cooked pasta

1. Place frozen chicken in slow cooker.
2. Add sliced onion and green peppers on top of chicken.
3. Mix together crushed tomatoes, tomato paste, garlic, Italian seasoning, salt and pepper, then pour sauce over chicken and veggies.
4. Cook 7 hours on low or 4-5 hours on high.
5. Serve over pasta with fresh Parmesan cheese.

SLOW COOKER ROASTED WHOLE CHICKEN

2½ tsps	salt
2 tsps	paprika
1 tsp	onion powder
½ tsp	garlic powder
½ tsp	black pepper
1	whole chicken (I usually look for the largest one I can find)

1. In small bowl, mix together first 5 ingredients.
2. Rinse chicken and pat dry.
3. Place whole chicken in slow cooker (be sure to remove the package of giblets from inside the bird prior to cooking).
4. Rub seasoning mixture into chicken.
5. Cook 5-8 hours on low, until chicken is cooked through and reaches an internal temperature of 180 degrees. Remove from slow cooker.
6. If you'd like to brown the skin a bit, cook under broiler in oven for about 5 minutes, until skin is golden brown.

daily grace

God is great, God is good ~ let us thank Him for our food.

CROCK-TOBER

VOLUME 2

CROCK-TOBER

VOLUME 2 • WEEK ONE

WEEK ONE GROCERY LIST

PRODUCE
- ☐ 3 onions
- ☐ 1 head garlic
- ☐ 1 lb fresh broccoli crowns
- ☐ 1 bunch celery
- ☐ bibb or iceberg lettuce
- ☐ 10 oz pkg shredded carrots
- ☐ 8 oz pkg sliced mushrooms

DAIRY
- ☐ ½ pint heavy cream
- ☐ 16 oz pkg shredded sharp cheddar cheese
- ☐ 4 oz pkg fresh shredded Parmesan cheese
- ☐ 4 oz tub blue, feta or goat cheese (your preference)

BUTCHER/DELI CASE/BAKERY
- ☐ 3½ lbs boneless, skinless chicken breasts, divided
- ☐ 2-3 lb shoulder roast (or favorite roast cut)

DRY/CANNED GOODS
- ☐ 2 12 oz cans evaporated milk
- ☐ 4 32 oz cartons low sodium chicken broth
- ☐ 12 oz bottle buffalo wing sauce
- ☐ 10 oz can enchilada sauce
- ☐ 4 oz can chopped green chiles
- ☐ 1 pkg taco seasoning (or homemade taco mix)
- ☐ 1 pkg taco shells or flour tortillas
- ☐ 16 oz pkg orzo pasta
- ☐ 15 oz can whole kernel corn
- ☐ 8 oz can artichoke hearts
- ☐ 14 oz can diced tomatoes

FROZEN
- ☐ 10 oz pkg frozen spinach

PANTRY STAPLES
- ☐ salt
- ☐ pepper
- ☐ honey
- ☐ low sodium soy sauce
- ☐ ketchup
- ☐ vegetable oil
- ☐ crushed red pepper flakes
- ☐ corn starch
- ☐ butter
- ☐ all purpose flour
- ☐ dried thyme
- ☐ ranch or blue cheese dressing

OPTIONAL
- ☐ sesame seeds (optional for Slow Cooker Honey Chicken)
- ☐ taco toppings (lettuce, tomato, cheese, sour cream, green onions)

SLOW COOKER HONEY CHICKEN

1 lb	boneless, skinless chicken breast
	salt and pepper
1 cup	honey
½ cup	low sodium soy sauce
¼ cup	ketchup
2 Tbsps	vegetable oil
½ cup	diced onion
¼ tsp	crushed red pepper flakes
2 cloves	garlic
	corn starch
	sesame seeds (optional)

1. Place chicken in slow cooker and season with salt and pepper.
2. Mix next seven ingredients in medium bowl and then pour over chicken.
3. Cover and cook on low 3-4 hours or 1½ hours on high.
4. Remove chicken from slow cooker and cut into pieces.
5. Meanwhile, mix 4 teaspoons corn starch in 6 teaspoons water, then pour into slow cooker.
6. Replace lid and cook sauce an additional ten minutes on high to thicken juices.
7. Return chicken to slow cooker to soak up the juices and warm. Sprinkle with sesame seeds, if desired.
8. Serve over noodles or rice.

daily grace
We thank the Lord for food and drink –
for appetite and power to think.
For loved ones dear – for home and friends –
for everything the good Lord sends.

SLOW COOKER BROCCOLI CHEESE SOUP

½ cup	butter
1½ cups	diced yellow onion
2 cloves	garlic, minced
6 Tbsps	all purpose flour
	salt and pepper
2 12 oz cans	evaporated milk
5 cups	low sodium chicken broth
5 cups	fresh broccoli florets
½ tsp	dried thyme
½ cup	heavy cream
3 cups	shredded sharp cheddar cheese
½ cup	fresh shredded Parmesan cheese

1. In large skillet melt butter over medium heat. Sauté onions until transparent, about 3-4 minutes.

2. Add garlic and flour, as well as a little salt and pepper to flavor; cook 2 minutes, stirring constantly.

3. Using a whisk, slowly add in evaporated milk and stir well to make smooth.

4. Cook mixture until it begins to thicken, then pour into slow cooker with chicken broth, broccoli and thyme.

5. Cover and cook on low 6 hours or 2½-3 hours on high.

6. Turn heat off (or warm if you have that option), and add in heavy cream, shredded cheddar cheese and Parmesan cheese.

7. Season with salt and pepper.

daily grace
For food and health and happy days
receive our gratitude and praise
In serving others Lord may we
Repay our depth of love to thee.

SLOW COOKER BUFFALO CHICKEN LETTUCE WRAPS

CHICKEN

1½ lbs	boneless, skinless chicken breasts
1 stalk	celery, cut in half
½	onion, sliced
2 cloves	garlic, minced
1½ cups	low sodium chicken broth
1 cup	buffalo wing sauce

1. Place chicken, celery stalk, onion, garlic and chicken broth in slow cooker.
2. Cover and cook on low 6 hours.
3. Remove chicken from slow cooker and shred.
4. Drain cooking liquid, reserving ½ cup; discard solids.
5. Toss chicken with reserved ½ cup broth.
6. Return to slow cooker and mix in wing sauce.
7. Cover and cook on low 30 more minutes.

WRAPS

	bibb or iceberg lettuce leaves
3 stalks	celery, chopped
1 cup	shredded carrots
	crumbled blue, feta or goat cheese
	ranch or blue cheese dressing

1. Fill lettuce leaves with chicken mixture and top with desired amount of celery, carrots, cheese and dressing.

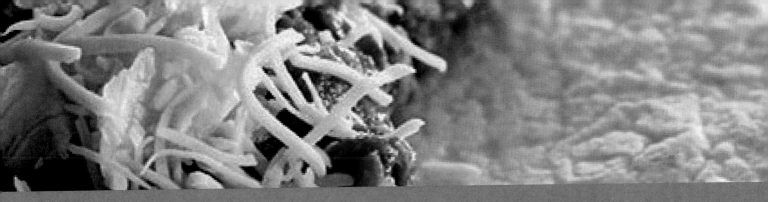

SLOW COOKER SHREDDED BEEF TACOS

10 oz can	enchilada sauce
4 oz can	chopped green chiles
2-3 lb	beef shoulder roast
1 pkg	taco seasoning (or homemade taco seasoning)
	taco shells or flour tortillas
	optional taco toppings (lettuce, tomato, cheese, sour cream, green onions)

1. Place roast in slow cooker.
2. Pour enchilada sauce, green chiles and taco seasoning on top of roast.
3. Cover and cook on low 8 hours.
4. Shred beef and serve on tacos.

SLOW COOKER CHICKEN MINESTRONE SOUP

1 cup	uncooked orzo pasta
1	onion, chopped
2 cloves	garlic, minced
2 32 oz cartons	low sodium chicken broth
15 oz can	whole kernel corn, undrained
8 oz can	artichoke hearts, drained
3 cups	cooked, shredded chicken
2 cups	sliced mushrooms
¾ tsp	salt
½ tsp	freshly ground black pepper
¾ tsp	crushed red pepper flakes
10 oz pkg	frozen spinach
14 oz can	diced tomatoes, drained
½ cup	fresh shredded Parmesan cheese

1. Place all ingredients except the Parmesan in the slow cooker (pasta does not need to be cooked).

2. Cover and cook on high 4-5 hours or low 7-8 hours.

3. Sprinkle with Parmesan and serve with crusty bread.

daily grace

For food and health and happy days
receive our gratitude and praise
In serving others Lord may we
Repay our depth of love to thee.

CROCK-TOBER

VOLUME 2 • WEEK TWO

WEEK TWO GROCERY LIST

PRODUCE
- ☐ 1 head garlic
- ☐ 4 large onions
- ☐ 1 red bell pepper
- ☐ 1 green bell pepper
- ☐ 3 carrots
- ☐ 1 bunch celery

DAIRY
- ☐ 6-8 oz pkg sliced provolone or Monterey Jack cheese
- ☐ 8 oz pkg shredded sharp cheddar cheese
- ☐ 1 dozen large eggs
- ☐ 4 oz pkg fresh shredded Parmesan cheese

BUTCHER/DELI CASE/BAKERY
- ☐ 2½-3 lb pork loin
- ☐ 1½ lbs boneless, skinless chicken breasts
- ☐ 2-3 lb beef sirloin tip roast
- ☐ 1 lb bacon
- ☐ 2 lbs ground beef
- ☐ 1 loaf Italian bread

DRY/CANNED GOODS
- ☐ 16 oz can black beans
- ☐ 2 16 oz cans red kidney beans
- ☐ 16 oz can white kidney beans
- ☐ 2 8 oz cans tomato sauce
- ☐ 2 28 oz cans diced tomatoes
- ☐ 2 10 oz cans Rotel
- ☐ 1 pkg taco seasoning (or homemade taco seasoning)
- ☐ 14 oz can low sodium beef broth
- ☐ 32 oz carton beef stock

- ☐ 24 oz jar spaghetti sauce
- ☐ 16 oz pkg ditalini pasta

FROZEN
- ☐ 10 oz pkg whole kernel corn
- ☐ 32 oz pkg hash browns

PANTRY STAPLES
- ☐ ground sage or thyme
- ☐ salt
- ☐ pepper
- ☐ brown sugar
- ☐ corn starch
- ☐ balsamic vinegar
- ☐ soy sauce
- ☐ chili powder
- ☐ teriyaki sauce
- ☐ vegetable oil
- ☐ Worcestershire sauce
- ☐ hot pepper sauce
- ☐ milk
- ☐ dry mustard
- ☐ cooking spray
- ☐ dried oregano
- ☐ dried parsley
- ☐ tabasco sauce

OPTIONAL
- ☐ breakfast casserole topping (green onions)
- ☐ chicken chili toppings (cheese, sour cream and tortilla chips)

SLOW COOKER BROWN SUGAR BALSAMIC GLAZED PORK LOIN

PORK

2½-3 lb	pork loin
1 tsp	ground sage or thyme
¼ tsp	pepper
½ tsp	salt
1 clove	garlic
½ cup	water

GLAZE

½ cup	brown sugar
1 Tbsp	corn starch
¼ cup	balsamic vinegar
½ cup	water
2 Tbsps	soy sauce

1. Mix together salt, pepper, garlic, and sage or thyme, adding about 1 Tablespoon water to make a paste.
2. Rub over pork loin.
3. Add ½ cup of water to slow cooker, place pork loin in slow cooker.
4. Cover and cook on low 6-8 hours.
5. An hour before the roast is finished, mix together the ingredients for the glaze in a small saucepan.
6. Cook over medium heat and stir about 4 minutes, until mixture thickens.
7. Brush roast with the glaze sauce every 20 minutes for the last hour of cooking.
8. Serve with remaining glaze on the side.

daily grace

For food that stays our hunger,
For rest that brings us ease,
For homes where memories linger,
We give our thanks for these.

SLOW COOKER CHICKEN TACO CHILI

1½ lbs	boneless, skinless chicken breasts
1 large	onion, chopped
16 oz can	black beans, drained and rinsed
16 oz can	red kidney beans, drained and rinsed
2 10 oz cans	Rotel
2 8 oz cans	tomato sauce
10 oz pkg	frozen whole kernel corn
1 pkg	taco seasoning (or homemade taco seasoning)
1 Tbsp	chili powder
	optional toppings (cheese, sour cream and tortilla chips)

1. Combine everything except optional toppings in slow cooker.
2. Cover and cook on low 7-8 hours or high 4-5 hours.
3. Once cooked, remove and shred chicken. Stir back in and cook another 10 minutes.
4. Serve with cheese, chips and sour cream, if desired.

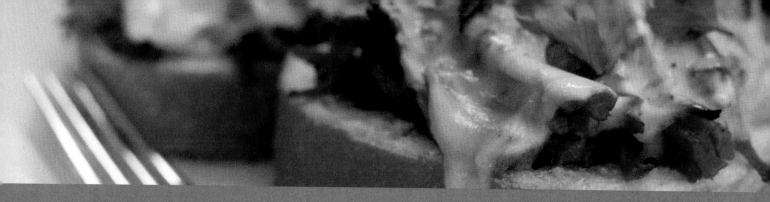

SLOW COOKER OPEN FACED SIRLOIN SANDWICHES

½ cup	teriyaki or soy sauce
½ cup	low sodium beef broth
¼ cup	vegetable oil
2 Tbsps	finely chopped onion
3 cloves	garlic, minced
2 Tbsps	brown sugar
1 tsp	Worcestershire sauce
½ tsp	hot pepper sauce
2-3 lbs	beef sirloin tip roast
	homemade bread or store bought Italian loaf, sliced thick and lightly toasted
	provolone or Monterey Jack cheese
	salt and pepper, to taste

1. Mix together teriyaki or soy sauce, beef broth, vegetable oil, onion, garlic, brown sugar, Worcestershire, and hot pepper sauce.

2. Place roast in a large zip-top bag, pour marinade over and refrigerate overnight.

3. In the morning, place roast and marinade in slow cooker. Cover and cook on low 7-8 hours.

4. Once beef is cooked, toast bread and place on baking sheet.

5. Layer shredded beef and provolone or Monterey Jack cheese on top of toasted bread.

6. Broil in oven 2-3 minutes, or until cheese is lightly browned.

daily grace
"So whether you eat or drink or whatever you do,
do it all for the glory of God."
1 Corinthians 10:31

SLOW COOKER PASTA FAGIOLI SOUP

2 lbs	ground beef
1	onion, chopped
3	carrots, peeled and chopped
4 stalks	celery, chopped
32 oz carton	beef stock
2 28 oz	diced tomatoes
24 oz jar	spaghetti sauce
16 oz can	red kidney beans, rinsed and drained
16 oz can	white kidney beans, rinsed and drained
3 tsps	oregano
2 tsps	pepper
5 tsps	parsley
1 tsp	Tabasco sauce, optional
8 oz	ditalini pasta (or other small pasta)
	freshly grated or shredded Parmesan cheese

1. Brown ground beef; drain and add to the slow cooker with everything except pasta.

2. Cover and cook on low 7-8 hours or high 4-5 hours.

3. When done, add pasta and cook an additional 30 minutes on high or 45 minutes on low.

4. Sprinkle with Parmesan cheese.

SLOW COOKER BREAKFAST CASSEROLE

1 lb	bacon
32 oz pkg	frozen hash brown potatoes, thawed
1	onion, diced
2 cloves	garlic, minced
1	red bell pepper, diced
1	green bell pepper, diced
8 oz pkg	shredded sharp cheddar cheese
12	eggs
1 cup	milk
1 tsp	dried mustard
	green onions, optional

1. Cook bacon; drain and crumble.

2. Coat slow cooker with cooking spray.

3. Spread half of the thawed hash browns in the bottom of slow cooker; then layer half of onion, garlic, bell peppers, cheese and bacon. Repeat with remaining hash browns, onion, garlic, bell peppers, cheese and bacon.

4. Whisk together eggs, milk, dried mustard and desired amount of salt and pepper until well combined.

5. Pour egg mixture over top; cover and cook on low 6-8 hours.

6. Top with sliced green onions, if desired.

NOTE: This recipe is so versatile and will work with breakfast sausage, link sausage, smoked sausage or diced ham. Top with sliced jalapeños, salsa, or hot sauce to spice things up!

daily grace

Christ our God, bless us Your servants,
our home, the food and drink before us for You are the
Source of all blessings, now and forever and ever. Amen.

CROCK-TOBER

VOLUME 2 ● WEEK THREE

WEEK THREE GROCERY LIST

PRODUCE
- ☐ 1 large and 1 small onion
- ☐ 1 green bell pepper
- ☐ 1 head garlic
- ☐ 1 medium-size broccoli crown
- ☐ 4-6 baking potatoes
- ☐ 1 bunch green onions

DAIRY
- ☐ 9 oz pkg refrigerated cheese tortellini
- ☐ 4 oz pkg fresh grated or shredded Parmesan cheese
- ☐ 8 oz carton sour cream
- ☐ 8 oz pkg shredded sharp cheddar cheese

BUTCHER/DELI CASE/BAKERY
- ☐ 4½-5½ lbs boneless, skinless chicken breasts, divided
- ☐ 1½ lbs ground beef

DRY/CANNED GOODS
- ☐ 1 packet reduced sodium chicken gravy
- ☐ 1 packet zesty Italian seasoning
- ☐ 4 14 oz cans low sodium beef broth
- ☐ 15 oz can Italian stewed tomatoes
- ☐ 1 jar picante sauce
- ☐ 12 oz bottle barbecue sauce
- ☐ 1 packet taco seasoning (or homemade taco seasoning)
- ☐ 4 oz can green chiles
- ☐ 10.75 oz can cream of chicken soup (or homemade cream of chicken soup)
- ☐ 10 oz can enchilada sauce
- ☐ 2.25 oz can sliced black olives
- ☐ 10-12 flour tortillas

PANTRY STAPLES
- ☐ smoked paprika
- ☐ salt/kosher salt
- ☐ corn starch
- ☐ pepper
- ☐ olive oil
- ☐ crushed basil leaves
- ☐ aluminum foil
- ☐ 2 eggs
- ☐ milk
- ☐ bread crumbs
- ☐ ketchup
- ☐ dry mustard
- ☐ garlic powder
- ☐ lime juice
- ☐ Italian salad dressing
- ☐ brown sugar
- ☐ worcestershire sauce
- ☐ cooking spray

OPTIONAL
- ☐ toppings for baked potatoes (cheese, sour cream, and chives)

SLOW COOKER CARMEN'S CHICKEN & GRAVY

1½ -2 lbs	boneless, skinless chicken breasts (or thighs)
1	reduced sodium chicken gravy packet
1	zesty Italian seasoning packet
14 oz can	low sodium beef broth
	smoked paprika and black pepper, to taste
	corn starch

1. Add chicken to slow cooker.

2. Mix packets with broth and pour over chicken. Sprinkle with desired amount of paprika and black pepper. Cover and cook on low 4-5 hours.

3. Thirty minutes prior to finishing, remove chicken, stir gravy to a nice even consistency and add a corn starch slurry consisting of 1 teaspoon corn starch and 2 teaspoons water.

4. Stir gravy after slurry addition to ensure a nice even consistency. Add shredded chicken to slow cooker and cook another 30 minutes on low.

5. Serve over warm mashed potatoes.

A special thank you to Passionate Penny Pincher reader Carmen for sharing this recipe with us ~ it's a favorite in our group and my family loved it too!

daily grace

*Bless this food to our use, us to your service
and bless the hands that prepared it.*

SLOW COOKER VEGETABLE TORTELLINI SOUP

1 large	onion, coarsely chopped
1 small	green bell pepper, chopped
2 cloves	garlic, minced
1 Tbsp	olive oil
3 14 oz cans	low sodium beef broth
15 oz can	Italian stewed tomatoes
½-¾ cup	picante sauce
1 tsp	crushed basil leaves
2 cups	fresh broccoli florets
9 oz pkg	refrigerated cheese tortellini
	freshly grated Parmesan cheese

1. Sauté onion, bell pepper and garlic in olive oil until tender.

2. Add to slow cooker along with beef broth, tomatoes, picante sauce and basil.

3. Cover and cook on low 5-6 hours or high 3 hours.

4. Increase heat to high; stir in broccoli and tortellini. Cover and cook 20-30 minutes or until pasta is tender.

5. Ladle into bowls and top with Parmesan cheese. Serve with crusty garlic bread.

SLOW COOKER BARBECUE STUFFED POTATOES

1½ – 2 lbs	boneless, skinless chicken breasts
12 oz bottle	barbecue sauce
½ cup	Italian salad dressing
¼ cup	brown sugar
2 Tbsps	Worcestershire sauce
4-6	baking potatoes
	toppings: cheese, sour cream, and chives (optional)

CHICKEN

1. Place chicken breast in bottom of slow cooker.
2. Mix together remaining four ingredients and pour on top of chicken.
3. Cover and cook on low 5-6 hours or high 3-4 hours.
4. Meanwhile bake potatoes in oven or bake in slow cooker.
5. Shred chicken and serve over potatoes. Add desired toppings.

POTATOES

1. Wash and thoroughly dry potatoes; prick all over with a fork.
2. Rub each potato with ½ teaspoon olive oil and sprinkle with kosher salt.
3. Wrap potatoes individually in aluminum foil.
4. Place in slow cooker; cover and cook on low 8-10 hours.

daily grace
"For he satisfies the thirsty
and fills the hungry with good things."
Psalm 107:9

SLOW COOKER CHICKEN ENCHILADAS

4-5	boneless, skinless chicken breasts
1 pkg	taco seasoning (or homemade taco seasoning)
1 tsp	garlic powder
4 oz can	green chiles
1 tsp	lime juice
¼ cup	water
10.75 oz can	cream of chicken soup (or homemade cream of chicken soup)
1 cup	sour cream
2 cups	shredded cheddar cheese
10 oz can	enchilada sauce
	green onions
	sliced olives
10-12	flour tortillas

1. Spray slow cooker with cooking spray.
2. Place chicken on bottom of slow cooker; add taco seasoning, garlic powder, green chiles, lime juice, and water.
3. Cover and cook on low 5-6 hours or high 3-4 hours.
4. Shred chicken.
5. Preheat oven to 350°F.
6. Mix together cream of chicken soup and sour cream.
7. Pour half of the sour cream mixture on the bottom of a 9 x 13-inch baking dish, and mix the other half in with the shredded chicken.
8. Place about ¼ cup chicken mixture and 2 tablespoons shredded cheese onto each tortilla.
9. Roll up and place seam side down in baking dish; repeat with remaining tortillas.
10. Pour enchilada sauce over the entire casserole and cover with remaining cheese; top with green onions and olives.
11. Cover with foil and bake 25 minutes. Remove foil and bake an additional 5 minutes.

SLOW COOKER MEATLOAF

1½ lbs	ground beef
2	eggs
¾ cup	milk
2/3 cup	bread crumbs
2 tsps	minced onion
1 tsp	salt
¼ cup	ketchup
2 Tbsps	brown sugar
1 tsp	dry mustard
½ tsp	Worcestershire sauce

1. Combine first six ingredients in large bowl; shape into loaf.

2. If you have a large slow cooker, put loaf in loaf pan and then place in slow cooker. You can cook this directly in a small slow cooker.

3. Cover and cook on low 5-6 hours.

4. Mix together ketchup, mustard, brown sugar and Worcestershire; spoon over meat loaf after it has cooked. Cook an additional 15 minutes, or until heated.

5. Let stand 10-15 minutes before slicing and serving. (Be sure to let it stand, otherwise it will fall apart very easily).

daily grace

Lord Jesus come now to our meal – and bless to us, this food.

Where faith is weak, dear Lord, reveal that all You give is good.

CROCK-TOBER

VOLUME 2 • WEEK FOUR

SLOW COOKER CHICKEN & SAUSAGE STEW

SLOW COOKER PESTO & RANCH CHICKEN

SLOW COOKER ROAST

SLOW COOKER PORK CACCIATORE

SLOW COOKER CHICKEN TORTILLA SOUP

PRODUCE
- ☐ 2 medium sweet potatoes
- ☐ 2 green bell peppers
- ☐ 1 red bell pepper
- ☐ 3 onions, divided
- ☐ 1 medium red onion
- ☐ 1 head garlic
- ☐ 2 large russet potatoes
- ☐ 8 oz pkg mushrooms

DAIRY
- ☐ 6-8 oz pkg sliced mozzarella cheese

BUTCHER/DELI CASE
- ☐ 1 lb pkg smoked sausage
- ☐ 4 lbs boneless, skinless chicken breasts, divided
- ☐ 3-4 lb beef shoulder roast
- ☐ 4-6 boneless pork chops

DRY/CANNED GOODS
- ☐ 15 oz can fire roasted diced tomatoes
- ☐ 2 15 oz cans diced tomatoes
- ☐ 32 oz carton chicken broth
- ☐ 32 oz carton beef broth
- ☐ 6 oz jar pesto sauce
- ☐ 1 packet ranch dressing mix (or homemade dry ranch dressing mix)
- ☐ 2 15 oz cans chicken broth
- ☐ 24 oz jar pasta sauce
- ☐ 10 oz can Rotel
- ☐ 10.75 oz can cream of chicken soup (or homemade cream of chicken soup)

- ☐ 15 oz can whole kernel corn
- ☐ 16 oz can black beans
- ☐ 1 bag tortilla chips
- ☐ 16 oz pkg angel hair pasta

FROZEN
- ☐ 12 oz pkg frozen chopped kale

PANTRY STAPLES
- ☐ salt
- ☐ pepper
- ☐ garlic powder
- ☐ hot sauce (such as Frank's)
- ☐ all purpose flour
- ☐ olive oil
- ☐ balsamic vinegar
- ☐ worcestershire sauce
- ☐ dijon mustard
- ☐ cubed beef bouillon
- ☐ dry white wine
- ☐ Italian seasoning
- ☐ dried basil
- ☐ chili powder
- ☐ ground cumin

OPTIONAL
- ☐ bread bowls (optional for Slow Cooker Roast)
- ☐ angel hair pasta or rice (optional for Slow Cooker Pesto & Ranch Chicken)
- ☐ grated Parmesan cheese (optional for Slow Cooker Pesto & Ranch Chicken)
- ☐ sour cream & shredded cheddar cheese (optional for Slow Cooker Chicken Tortilla Soup)

SLOW COOKER CHICKEN & SAUSAGE STEW

1 lb pkg	smoked sausage, sliced into bite sized pieces and browned
2-3	boneless, skinless chicken breasts (or use shredded meat from a rotisserie chicken)
2 medium	sweet potatoes, peeled and diced
1	red bell pepper diced
1	green bell pepper, diced
1	onion, diced
15 oz can	fire roasted diced tomatoes
15 oz can	diced tomatoes
32 oz carton	chicken broth
12 oz pkg	frozen chopped kale
1 tsp	garlic powder
	hot sauce to taste, about 8-10 shakes

1. Combine browned sausage and remaining ingredients in slow cooker.

2. Cover and cook on low 8 hours.

3. Serve with extra hot sauce, if desired.

daily grace

Christ our God, bless us Your servants, our home,
the food and drink before us for You are the
Source of all blessings, now and forever and ever. Amen.

SLOW COOKER PESTO & RANCH CHICKEN

2 lbs	boneless, skinless chicken breasts
6 oz	jar pesto sauce
1 packet	ranch dressing mix (or homemade ranch dressing mix)
1 cup	chicken broth
	angel hair pasta or rice (optional)
	grated Parmesan cheese (optional)

1. Place chicken in slow cooker.
2. Spread pesto over chicken and sprinkle with ranch dressing mix.
3. Pour chicken broth into slow cooker.
4. Cover and cook on low 4-6 hours.
5. It's delicious alone, or served over pasta or rice and sprinkled with Parmesan cheese.

SLOW COOKER ROAST

3-4 lb	beef shoulder roast
3 Tbsps	flour
1 tsp	salt
2½ tsps	pepper
2 Tbsps	olive oil
1 medium	red onion, thinly sliced
6 cloves	garlic, minced
2 large	russet potatoes, cut into ¼" slices
32 oz carton	beef broth
2 Tbsps	balsamic vinegar
2 Tbsps	Worcestershire sauce
1 Tbsp	Dijon mustard
1 Tbsp	small cube beef bouillon
1 cup	water
	bread bowls (optional)

1. Rinse roast and pat dry.
2. Cut a 1-inch "X" on top of roast-not slicing all the way through the roast but enough to leave room for the onions to set down in the roast.
3. Mix together flour, salt and 1 teaspoon pepper.
4. Coat roast in flour mixture and cook in oil 2 minutes until each side is lightly browned.
5. Place roast in slow cooker.
6. Stuff onion and garlic down into the roast; adding carrots and onions around the roast.
7. Mix together beef broth, vinegar, Worcestershire, mustard, beef bouillon, water and 1½ teaspoons pepper.
8. Pour broth mixture over roast; cover and cook on low 8-10 hours.
9. Pour into bread bowls, if desired.

daily grace

For good food and those who prepare it,
for good friends with whom to share it, we thank you Lord. Amen.

SLOW COOKER PORK CACCIATORE

4-6	boneless pork chops
2 Tbsps	olive oil
1	onion, sliced
8 oz pkg	fresh mushrooms, sliced
1	green bell pepper, seeded and sliced into strips
24 oz jar	pasta sauce
15 oz can	diced tomatoes
½ cup	dry white wine or chicken broth
1 tsp	Italian seasoning
½ tsp	dried basil
2 large	cloves garlic, minced
4 slices	mozzarella cheese
16 oz pkg	angel hair pasta, cooked

1. Lightly brown pork chops in olive oil over medium-high heat.

2. Place pork chops in slow cooker.

3. Cook onion in same pan as pork chops over medium heat until browned; add in mushrooms and bell pepper cooking until vegetables are tender.

4. Add pasta sauce, diced tomatoes, and white wine or chicken broth; season with Italian seasoning, basil, and garlic.

5. Pour tomato mixture over pork chops.

6. Cover and cook on low 7-8 hours.

7. Serve over cooked pasta, and top with mozzarella cheese.

SLOW COOKER CHICKEN TORTILLA SOUP

2-3 cups	shredded cooked chicken
10 oz can	Rotel
14 oz can	chicken broth
10.75 oz can	cream of chicken soup (or homemade cream of chicken soup)
15 oz can	whole kernel corn, drained
16 oz can	black beans, drained and rinsed
½ tsp	chili powder
¼ tsp	ground cumin
½ tsp	garlic powder
¼ cup	chopped onion
	tortilla chips
	sour cream and shredded cheddar cheese, optional

1. Add first ten ingredients to slow cooker.
2. Cover and cook on low 6-8 hours.
3. Place tortilla chips in bowls. Pour soup over tortilla chips, adding cheddar cheese and sour cream, if desired.

daily grace
Lord Jesus, thank you for this day,
And for the night of rest,
And for this food, and for the way
That we are always blessed.

CROCK-TOBER
ADDITIONAL RESOURCES

HOMEMADE CREAM OF CHICKEN SOUP

2 cups	nonfat dry milk
¾ cup	corn starch
¼ cup	low sodium instant chicken bouillon granules
1 tsp	dry onion powder
1 tsp	dried basil
½ tsp	pepper

1. Mix together all ingredients.
2. Store at room temperature in plastic bag or container.
3. To use, mix together 1/3 cup dry mixture with 1 ¼ cups water to make 1 can cream of chicken soup.

HOMEMADE TACO SEASONING PACKET

2 tsps	chili powder
½ tsp	salt
½ tsp	garlic powder
½ tsp	cumin
¼ tsp	pepper
1½ tsps	paprika
1 tsp	onion powder
	pinch red pepper flakes

1. Mix all ingredients, equals one package taco seasoning mix.

ADDITIONAL RESOURCES

HOMEMADE DRY RANCH DRESSING SEASONING PACKET

¾ tsp	black pepper
1 tsp	seasoning salt
1 tsp	dried parsley
½ tsp	garlic powder
¼ tsp	onion powder

1. Mix all ingredients, equals one package ranch dressing seasoning mix.

HOMEMADE ITALIAN DRESSING SEASONING PACKET

1½ tsps	garlic powder
1 Tbsp	onion powder
2 Tbsps	Italian seasoning
1 Tbsp	sugar
2 Tbsps	salt
1 tsp	black pepper

1. Mix all ingredients and store at room temperature in plastic bag or container.
2. To use, mix 2 tablespoons in place of seasoning packet.

BEST BREAD MACHINE DOUGH

1 cup	warm water (110 – 115°F)
1 Tbsp	milk
2 Tbsps	oil
2 Tbsps	honey
2 Tbsps	brown sugar
1 tsp	salt
3 cups	all purpose flour
2 tsps	instant active dry yeast or active dry yeast

1. Put ingredients in the order above into bread machine (you don't need to stir it, just dump it in!)

2. Set bread machine on dough setting, and let it make the dough for you.

3. Once dough is made (it takes my machine about 1½ hours to make), remove dough and place in loaf pan.

4. Let rise for about 30 minutes to an hour if you have time – sometimes when I don't I just go ahead and bake it and it works out fine.

5. Bake in 350°F oven for 30 minutes.

BEST CHOCOLATE CHIP COOKIES {EVER}

2 cups	flour
1 tsp	baking soda
1 tsp	salt
1 cup	white sugar
½ cup	light brown sugar
1 cup	shortening
2	eggs
1 tsp	vanilla
12 oz	chocolate chips

1. Preheat oven to 375°F.
2. Cream shortening and sugars together until well blended.
3. Add eggs and vanilla, mix well. In separate bowl combine flour, baking soda and salt. Mix with spoon, then add to shortening mixture and mix until well blended.
4. Add chocolate chips.
5. Bake in 375°F oven for 7-9 minutes.
6. When you pull them out of the oven lightly tap the pan on your counter top to "settle" your cookies. Let cool on wire rack.

daily grace
Bless the food before us ~
the family beside us ~ and the love between us.

Made in the USA
Middletown, DE
19 October 2017